IF YOU DO THE DIFFICULT,
GOD WILL DO THE

IMPOSSIBLE

IF YOU DO THE DIFFICULT, GOD WILL DO THE
IMPOSSIBLE

JEAN CASSIDY

Pleasant Word
A Division of WINEPRESS PUBLISHING

Pleasant Word (a division of WinePress Publishing, PO Box 428, Enumclaw, WA 98022) functions only as book publisher. As such, the ultimate design, content, editorial accuracy, and views expressed or implied in this work are those of the author.

Unless otherwise indicated, all Scriptures are taken from the *Good News Translation Bible* (GNT). Copyright 1966, 1976 by American Bible Society. This translation is known as the *Good News Bible* (GNB) around the world.

ISBN 1-4141-0751-X
Library of Congress Catalog Card Number: 2006903416

Jesus said, "What is impossible with men is possible with God" (Luke 18:27 NIV).

DEDICATION

When I became aware that it was time to dedicate this book, I thought of the Lord Jesus Himself. I wish to dedicate *If You Do the Difficult, God Will Do the Impossible* to Jesus and to thank Him for all He has done for me and mine.

TABLE OF CONTENTS

Acknowledgements   XI

Introduction   XIII

1. Jean's Story   15

2. Some of the Behaviors You May Want
   to Change   23

3. The Beginning of the Difficult   25

4. Letting Go of Others   33

5. The Blame Game   37

6. Victimization   41

7. Dealing with Resentments   45

8. Shame   49

9. Seeing Myself Through the Eyes of Others   53

10. Loving Myself   57

11. My God/Our God   63
12. Unrealistic Expectations   65
13. Judgment   71
14. Stealing Blessings   73
15. How to Be Real   77
16. Grace for Today   81
17. Parenting   85
18. Twelve Steps of Recovery   93
19. Taking a Personal Inventory   105
20. Some of Our God-given Gifts   111
21. Understanding Alcoholism   113
22. Understanding Codependency   115
23. Sobriety   119

ACKNOWLEDGEMENTS

I wish to thank my editor, Marylane Wade Koch, whom the Lord definitely put in my life. I want to thank her for all of her work and her prayers. Without her help this book would not have come to pass.

I also want to acknowledge my husband Scotty who has been encouraging in all of my efforts. My family has been so supportive: my daughter Sharon for all of her assistance, my grandson Colton for all of his help, and my sons-in-law Carney and Mike. Thank you all for your computer knowledge.

I am so thankful for all of you. I want to thank all my prayer warriors—you know who you are.

Thank you all.

God bless, Jean

INTRODUCTION

If you could purchase a road map to a healthy life, would you do it? The mission of this book is to help anyone who desires spiritual and emotional wellness. Having wandered the unhealthy path and having been redirected to the healthy highway, my heart's desire is to assist others to find wholeness for their life journeys.

Turning my life over to the Lord Jesus Christ was the healthiest choice I ever made, though not an easy one. I had to accept that my will was the only possession I had to turn over to the Lord God. Everything else was His anyway. However, this decision had to be by my free will or it would not be sincere. This process did not occur all at once for me. I learned that when I acted in my own will, I made a mess of things. This behavior is particularly true for those who are "self-will-run-riot people," a phrase I would later understand as I left my old ways behind.

For many years I have wanted to write this book. I procrastinated, deluding myself by saying I was waiting for the Lord God to tell me when to begin. In fact, He told me some time ago to write my insights and share them with others. So here I am, finally doing the bidding of my Heavenly Father.

Please share with me as I make amends to my Lord God for my hesitation and for my disobedience to His bidding:

"I am sorry, Father, for not being more open to Your bidding. I commit to putting all of my effort into this work on Your behalf. I ask for a blessing on this work, Father. Everything I am about to write was taught to me by You. I desire for this book to be a testimony to the faithfulness of my Lord and Savior Jesus Christ."

Chapter 1

JEAN'S STORY

June 1957, marked my arrival in America. A wealthy family sponsored me to be a nanny to their five children and to help with the housework. I was so lonely without my large family of four brothers, a sister, my mom, and my dad. Sometimes I believed I had made a mistake in leaving my family in Scotland. Thoughts of returning to Scotland surfaced, but I decided to stay to attend a friend's wedding. This is when I began to see the hand of God in my life.

At my friend's wedding, I met my husband to be, also from Scotland. When we started dating, I postponed my return home. After a while, our relationship became serious, and I no longer wanted to return to Scotland.

He was the right man for me—I was in love! We both wrote to our families and encouraged them to connect.

To their surprise, they found that they had known each other for many years. My new love and I had so much in common: we had even arrived in America on the same day, he by air and I by sea. We shared the same religion and we seemed to believe all the same things. Everything appeared destined to happen. Our marriage was blessed on May 29, 1959.

In our happiness, we started a family right away. Our first daughter Elizabeth was born in April 1960, followed by Jim in August 1962. Sharon was the next child, born in April 1965, and then came baby daughter Carol, in February 1968.

The beginning years of our marriage were storybook. We enjoyed each other and our babies. Then something happened that changed our close-to-perfect life together: the disease of alcoholism reared its ugly head.

Yes, we often drank alcohol. However, my husband's drinking was getting out of control. He now drank every night. He joined a men's club which took even more of his time away from home and afforded him more drinking opportunities.

The more my husband drank, the more excuses I made for him. When he was angry with the children, I would tell them he was sick. When he could not go to work, I called his employer to report he was ill. Responsibilities he once assumed I now managed alone. Covering his behavior became my focus. My motive was to "keep peace" in our home. Not once did I blame his drinking. I reasoned that if he would do his drinking at home, everything would be all right. My denial regarding his alcohol addiction remained strong.

What I now understand is that I was too afraid to see the problem, thinking I was the problem. I thought our relationship issues were because I was not "enough" wife to my husband nor "enough" mother to our children. Now I see that my thinking helped him to keep the drinking going, a behavior called *enabling,* a destructive pattern. I engaged in this behavior for many years and through many hard times.

In 1970, after eleven years of marriage and really difficult times, my husband decided to look into his problem. Subsequently he began attending 12-step meetings, found sobriety, and accepted the fact that he was an alcoholic. More than thirty-six years later he is still sober, thanks be to God!

In the 1960s and 1970s, I had no relationship with the Lord Jesus Christ. Yes, I had "religion," which had no power to help me. The Scripture says in 2 Timothy 3:5 (NIV), *"having a form of godliness but denying its power. Have nothing to do with them."* That was me. I held up an image of godliness, but it was empty.

Life as it was continued. Someone suggested I attend Al-Anon, a 12-step program for spouses and others who had been or were affected by someone else's drinking. In Al-Anon, I found and owned my problem. Like my husband, I also had unhealthy behaviors that needed revision. Although I refrained from social drinking, my issues emerged, such as my addiction or obsession to my husband and his behavior. Making my husband stop drinking had become my job. In addition I was totally dependent on his opinion and on his approval to validate myself. Like any addiction, it left me unfulfilled. There was never enough validation because I was looking for it in the wrong place.

My own beliefs controlled me. If my husband had a bad day, I had a bad day. I was completely enmeshed with my husband who was enmeshed with alcohol. Essentially, alcohol owned both our lives. What an eye opener that was! I mistakenly believed I was free of any defects, which shows how much I needed healing. By accepting the awareness I was being given, and attempting to apply the principles to myself, the journey to wellness began.

After a year of sobriety my husband and I found ourselves in distress. Although he was working his program and staying alcohol free, he continued to show signs of emotional immaturity, typical with this disease. These behaviors had an impact on our marriage and our household. Repeated manipulation, dishonesty, and verbal and emotional abuse occurred in addition to negative outside influences. He and I decided to separate. Neither of us knew God, so we had no healthy value system upon which to build our lives.

This was a terrifying time for me. I was a mother with four children and my family was in Scotland. My self-confidence and self-esteem were at their lowest. I honestly thought I could not exist without my husband. But during this time, my awareness of how much I needed God grew. I remember crying out: "God, if you are there, please save me!" not knowing what to expect. About this time, I started to feel hope. God taught me to stand on my own two feet and to do what I knew was right. I began owning my part in my predicament. I still did not know God, but I had begun to seek Him. I read everything I could find, except the Word of God. My previous religion taught me that ordinary people were not clever enough to read the Bible—that clergy were the only ones who could do that. My seeking continued.

Attending Al-Anon, I learned about myself. This insight clearly showed me that I had not been living my own life but living life for others. I was not even present in my own life. More aware of everything outside of myself, I never knew what was going on inside me, such as my feelings, my wants, my beliefs—anything to do with me and my well being. It was an awful place to be. When healing began, I learned that God has given each of us permission to love ourselves, not just others. In fact, He said, *"…love your neighbor as yourself"* in Leviticus 19:18 (NIV). I had never loved myself but felt contempt for myself, always feeling "less" than everyone else.

Gratefully, now I know I am not less, and not more, than any other human being. As I learned more about myself, I actually started to like me. Without the emotional enmeshment with my husband, I was able to work on my issues and to deal with my own faults and sin.

After about a year of separation, my husband relocated from New York to Florida. He invited me down to visit him for possible reconciliation. Clearly, both of us had matured and both wanted to recommit to our marriage. When the children finished school for the summer, we moved to Florida to reunite with their father and become a family again.

"So," one might ask, "Was it happily ever after?" Unfortunately, problems continued and often I wondered if we should have moved to Florida. Some people in New York advised me not to reconcile. Many issues still needed resolution. How could I allow my husband to have authority over our household and the children and trust him again? Depression set in as I missed my friends and other support persons. My husband and I began to ask ourselves, "Is this sobriety? Is this all there is?" During this challenging time we began to see our need for God. As we prayed and asked God to show Himself to us, He did.

One night, while watching television, I became interested in a program called *The 700 Club*. I tried to dismiss my interest by calling them "Bible thumpers." I did not even know what that term meant, but I had heard others say it. In the following weeks I tuned into that program several times. Even when I was not looking for it, this program just seemed to appear whenever I turned on the television. One particular night, a lady with a British accent was on the program. She said that she was married to an alcoholic who was in recovery. Some of her journey included the loneliness and resentment that she had carried with her. She thought about taking her own life because her life had been empty. The coping mechanisms she employed were not helping her. She thought that her husband's sobriety would be the answer to all of her problems, but then she realized that was not the case. Her life was still not healthy.

This woman was telling my story, speaking to my heart. She had been led to the Lord Jesus Christ, who saved her, and now He was the center of her life. She went on to say, "If anyone out there is listening to me and wants this peace and love that I have found, go down on you knees and repeat after me, 'Jesus I am lost; I am a sinner. I have sinned against you and myself. Jesus, please forgive me. Come into my heart and be my Savior and my God and I will follow you all the days of my life.'" That night in 1976 I asked Jesus to come into my heart and be my Savior and my God. He did and my life has never been the same. Thank you, Lord. I realized that God had been teaching me about Himself before I even knew who He was. That is so like God!

I began to pray for my husband and about six months later he received Jesus Christ as his Lord and Savior. Today we are blessed to walk in the love of Jesus Christ. The Bible says, *"...call upon me in the day of trouble; I will deliver you, and you will honor me"* (Psalm 50:15 NIV).

Chapter 2

SOME OF THE BEHAVIORS YOU MAY WANT TO CHANGE

"If you are wise, your wisdom will reward you; if you are a mocker, you alone will suffer."

—Proverbs 9:12 NIV

Each person needs to examine his/her own behaviors to improve spiritual and emotional health. Below is a list of suggestions that I personally found important:

<u>How not to pray</u>: Do not ask God to change other people so you can be comfortable. Do not ask Him to take away the storms in your life (some of these are not even real).

<u>How to pray</u>: Ask God to change you, to help you be more like Him. Ask God to give you peace in the middle of the storm, to help you see the truth, and to become real.

How not to communicate: Do not try to make other people feel guilty. Do not manipulate others. Do not tell others what you think they want to hear.

How to communicate: Be honest with yourself and with others. Express yourself in a loving way. Be yourself for the sake of yourself, not to pressure other people to change.

How not to shame yourself: Remember, no labels, no believing you are not worthy, no convincing others you are not worthy, and no victimization. Be willing to do what you must do to be healthy. If nothing changes, nothing changes.

How not to feel sorry for yourself: Unless you like feeling sorry for yourself, which some people do, it can be a perfect excuse for not changing. It has "tow" effects, meaning it drains life from you. No blessing is available for people who feel sorry for themselves. The way of escape is to find an "attitude of gratitude."

How not to procrastinate: Do not put things off until tomorrow. We begin to feel accomplished and not ruled by our fears if we live "in the now." We do the things of the day. Be kind to yourself. Do not procrastinate about your procrastination. Those who procrastinate lose out.

Chapter 3

THE BEGINNING
OF THE DIFFICULT

"God, Grant me the serenity to accept the things I cannot change, Courage to change the things I can, And the Wisdom to know the difference."
—The Serenity Prayer:

When I first learned that prayer, I thought good things would happen if I said the prayer often enough. What I would eventually learn is that there are times when I have to do the difficult before God will do the impossible. Here are the insights I have been blessed to learn.

God, grant me the serenity to accept the things I cannot change.

What is it I cannot change? I can change only my own behavior. I cannot change another person; only that person can change his or her own behavior. In order to make changes, I first had to look critically at my own behavior, for instance my need to get my loved ones to do what I thought was best. I thought I knew what was right for them. It did not really matter whether I was correct or not; I thought it was my responsibility to make other people do what I thought was right.

In addition to causing dissension in my relationships, my behavior cost me my peace of mind. I was unable to look at my own sins of control and self-righteousness.

When I learned that I was expected to apply the Serenity Prayer, I realized it was up to me to ask God to give me the serenity to accept others. In order to do that, I had to ask God to give me the willingness to do so. That seemed impossible for me because I had never been able to let go of my need to be "right." God made that possible for me to do. I learned to sometimes give up the right to be right, though not always. I make the choice when I am willing to do so.

There are many opportunities in life when something or someone is difficult to accept. Although others may not agree, I think a healthy person must learn to accept people for who they are and not try to change them. In the same way, I am not responsible to be who others want me to be. I continue to pray for others, praying for the Father's will for them, not my will.

God grant me the courage to change the things I can.

My first task on the road to health was to look at what I needed to change. Boy, was that scary! I was not sure what I would find. Being honest with myself was difficult. Again I asked the Lord God to make me willing to be honest. He did, and I identified my shortcomings, my sin nature. After identifying the things that were dishonest in me, I asked the Lord to give me the courage to be disciplined and faithful to deal with those issues. For instance, there were times when I had to discipline my tongue when I would have been sarcastic. I learned that the root of the word "sarcastic" means "to cut a piece of flesh (from the targeted person)." I did not want to tear anyone's flesh; I just thought I was being clever. In actuality, I was being cruel. I was not healthy enough to honestly express myself.

In addition, I was also filled with self-pity. What a terrible twosome! God gave me the courage to change the things I could. I was able to take my shortcomings to Him in honesty, with a willingness to have them removed.

*"Then I acknowledged my sin to you and did not cover
up my iniquity. I said, 'I will confess my transgressions
to the LORD—and you forgave the guilt of my sin."*
—Psalm 32:5 NIV

Another thing I discovered about myself was that
I had learned to "stuff my feelings." I was unable to be
honest about my feelings because I could not identify
them. I had to actually learn what I felt. For instance,
how did I "feel" about feeling I was somehow inad-
equate? How did I "feel" about being emotionally and
verbally abused? I did not know how I felt. I did not
understand that it was healthy to express feelings. Since
then I have learned that it is necessary to feel and express
those feelings when I need to or want to. Feelings are
given by God and help keep me emotionally healthy.
This is not about opinions but feelings, an expression of
myself. I had lost my willingness to express myself and
became self-contemptuous in the process.

God taught me to be free to express myself, sometimes in pleasure and sometimes in displeasure, but always to be spoken in love and honesty. God also showed
me that I had to deal with my need to "people-please"
before I could express myself with honesty.

God grant me the wisdom to know the difference.

What difference? What was my responsibility and
what was the other person's responsibility? Where did I

end and where did someone else begin? This is an age-old question. Personal boundaries are important for many reasons. First, how can I be responsible for my own sin if I blame someone else? Secondly how can I ask God to direct my path if I do not know who I am or when I am emotionally enmeshed with another? I realized that thinking of others every waking moment and depending on them to fulfill my needs is idolatry; those persons or things were my god. To be healthy, I had to know the difference!

I learned to respect the people in my life yet allow them to walk their own journey. Now I can love others the way God loves me. He has never assumed the blame for my selfish actions or their consequences. He does not stop me from falling down, but He allows me to experience the consequences of my actions, both healthy and unhealthy. God allows me to grow from these events, yet I know He is always there for me. He is always willing to forgive me and welcome me back.

God gave me the wisdom to know the difference. Now I know who I am and I know what He wants me to do. He wants me to be all that He made me to be, and He wants that for each person on this earth, too.

"But seek first his kingdom and his righteousness, and all these things will be given to you as well."
—Matthew 6:33 NIV

What "things" does this mean? "These things" include spiritual health, peace, acceptance of reality, grace, understanding, compassion, love of self, love of others, love of God, kindness, patience, humility, gentleness, wisdom, delight, joy, and so much more. The "difficult" is the seeking. The "impossible" is having all these things added to me. God is the only One who can do that.

Did I want to be healed? In John 5:6 (NIV), the story of the paralytic, an invalid for thirty-eight years, reads, "*When Jesus saw him lying there and learned that he had been in this condition for a long time, he asked him, 'Do you want to get well?'*" In John 5:8 (NIV), Jesus told him "*…Get up! Pick up your mat and walk.*"

I wonder what this man was thinking? What did this man do? Did he want to be healed? Of course, and so did I. What I heard Jesus asking is, "Do you want to give up all the things you have come to depend on, the people who have been carrying you around, the people who have been feeding you, your self-pity, and any other strategies you may depend on?"

I find that people have behaviors that they may not want to let go of. Holding on can block restoration to spiritual and emotional health.

What behaviors might a person choose to "use?" One person may work to excess, being a "workaholic." This behavior can help someone avoid personal needs and issues. Sometimes people believe they should be able to fix anything in their lives in their own strength, not trusting the Lord God, not allowing God to be God. Another person may be trying to be "all things to all people." Can I accept my own limitations or my own unique value in God? Do I make other people the center of my life? Do I look to these people or things to fulfill my needs? Many strategies are used. Examining my behaviors and motives can identify the issues that I use to keep myself unhealthy so that I can then find new ways to become healthy.

About fourteen years ago, I was diagnosed with arteriosclerosis and was prescribed a cholesterol reduction drug. Apparently the drugs were ineffective for me because several months later a heart bypass procedure for my occluded arteries was necessary. I entered the hospital somewhat apprehensive but not overly concerned because lots of people told me it was an everyday occurrence—nothing to be concerned about.

The procedure was successful and I was taken to ICU, the normal procedure. Shortly afterwards, I developed a problem. The new arteries in my chest detached. Fortunately, I was still under anesthesia. The emergency response team on the hospital staff was notified. My surgeon, who was still at the hospital, came to my aid. The team opened my chest right there in the ICU as they attempted to reattach the grafts.

After seventeen units of blood and several strategies to restore cardiac function, my heart was still not responding. My husband and children were told I might not survive, and even if I did, I possibly could spend the rest of my days in a vegetative state. In fact, my family was encouraged to say their good-byes to me, which they did. As family and friends prayed for my recovery that Friday, I was oblivious to what was going on. On Monday I awakened to find out about my adventures.

While I was under anesthesia, I was in the valley of the shadow of death. I believe I was being prepared to go before the Most High God. I did not see any lights and there was no tunnel, as some have reported in near death experiences. What I did feel was Agape Love—God's love. I felt deep love for every living thing that my eyes could see. Later I realized that I had been touched by God. I could only feel that kind of love by God's hand. I prayed for wellness and God honored those prayers. *And the prayer offered in faith will make the sick person well; the Lord will raise him up* (James 5:15 NIV).

I am most thankful for the prayer warriors in my life. Fourteen years later, I am still doing well. *"Do not be afraid, little flock, for your Father has been pleased to give you the kingdom"* (Luke 12:32 NIV).

Chapter 4

LETTING GO OF OTHERS

How did I let go of loved ones and still care for them? First I understood that I was not giving up, but rather letting go emotionally and allowing others to live their lives. I came to realize that I am not to control another human being, try to "fix" others, or make others do what makes me comfortable. I began to "Let Go and Let God." To let God handle this meant I had to come to believe that He is the only One who can "fix" or heal the person or situation.

To gain the awareness that God is the only One who can "fix," I had to take a personal inventory. One example of my inventory applied to my need to control. First I had to sort out exactly what was my responsibility. I had believed that somehow I was responsible for the people I loved and for their behaviors. Yet how could I be responsible for others' behaviors or their sins? This inventory was not easy for me. But I remembered that I was called to do the difficult. I looked at the issues that caused me the most trouble: dealing with others and their behaviors. When I did not agree with the actions of the people in my life, I tried to make them see how wrong they were, always thinking my way was right.

Something that helped me during this time was keeping a journal. I wrote down all my thoughts. Later I was able to see some of my twisted ideas. Some of my expectations were unrealistic. I was not experiencing my own life; I was always thinking about tomorrow or fretting about yesterday. I was seldom in the present—the "now." But God is in the now, and I learned that I could choose to stay in the now.

To let go is freeing—so freeing that I was able to acquire the willingness and the energy to become what God wanted me to be. I discovered that "Letting go" is different from "giving up." "Letting go" means I no longer take responsibility for another person's sins or behaviors. I was to deal with my own feelings and behaviors. "Letting go" meant I had enough respect to trust that the person I was concerned about would deal with his or her own issues. If that person chooses not to do so, that decision belongs to them. Letting go is difficult; it is difficult to trust other people to be responsible. Realizing that I am not God is difficult. But I had to come to see that God is God; I am not.

I learned to let people own their personal issues, to become responsible for them, and to see that "letting go" is the most loving action I can take, in addition to praying. I am not giving up on others, but I am giving them to the Lord God.

I've found that God gives me the measure of grace I need each day. He even told me *"...My grace is sufficient for you..."* (2 Corinthians 12:19 NIV). However, at times God's grace somehow did not seem to be sufficient for me. I believed God's Word is absolute, therefore I reasoned I must be doing something wrong. I asked the Lord God to show me my error, and He did: I was using my daily grace on yesterday and tomorrow.

Some of my worries were not even my own. *"Therefore do not worry about tomorrow, for tomorrow will worry about itself. Each day has enough trouble of its own"* (Matthew 6:34 NIV). "Stay in the now" is what I learned; "stay in the now" to fully enjoy God's grace.

Sometimes I wanted other people, particularly those I love, to live their lives the way I thought they should. I would find myself thinking, "If they would just do what I tell them to do, everything would be fine." Now when I see that I am trying to run other people's lives, I identify the issue of control. This is ludicrous when I think about it. Since I was not doing such a great job of running my own life, how could I possibly run someone else's life?

Sometimes in a relationship I am better served to give up the right to be right. I ask myself, "How important is this issue?" If it is an issue of integrity, faithfulness, or some other part of my value system, then, of course, I stand on my convictions. However, if it is a relatively trivial matter, and there are many of those each day, then it becomes necessary to weigh the situation and ask, "How important is it?"

Chapter 5

THE BLAME GAME

Whether emotional, mental, physical, or sexual, abuse comes in many forms. Abuse causes damage to the inner person. When people experience abuse, they are often left with a damaged self-esteem. Any abuse leaves a victim just waiting to be revictimized. In fact people often re-victimize themselves by revisiting the abuse experience again and again. The *difficult* in this situation would be to pursue professional help to heal the damage from abuse. But to give oneself permission to be healthy can in itself be difficult. Healthy people know how to ask for what they need; victims seldom do. Healthy people are kind to themselves and get help. They ask for what they need.

I was a victim. Because I was a victim, I allowed myself to be victimized over and over again. When I finally got help, I learned I was actually teaching people how to treat me. By allowing myself to be hurt again and again, by accepting unacceptable behavior from others, I realized that I was in a "less than" mode. What a blessing to be able to see this and have a way of escape. I am blessed. I am willing to see the truth.

Blaming other people for the negative circumstances in life is not healthy. But there is a way of escape. For some, like me, the blame game comes easily. With so many wounds, it is difficult not to place blame on the person or the situation that inflicted the wound. However, I saw that I must take ownership for the wound. The pain is mine; I own it. The only road to recovery is to look at what the pain has cost, grieve that loss, and prepare to forgive those people who did the wounding.

The only way for me to forgive was to ask the Lord God to give me a heart of forgiveness, to be obedient to His will, and to remember that each wounding person has been forgiven just as I, also a wounding person, have been forgiven. If a person blames others because life is not what it should be, perceptions will probably never change. Each person must take responsibility for his or her own feelings and behaviors. This means no more saying, "It's because of him, or her, or them, that I feel this way." Giving others power over one's emotional state only keeps that person in bondage.

If a person thinks, "If only they would be different, I could be happy," he or she must face this fact: this is not true. If someone is not happy now, it is because of himself or herself, at least in part. Each person has to decide to receive happiness. Abraham Lincoln said, "I knew a man who had a terrible life and most of it never happened." That man was in the bondage of negative thinking.

The Scripture teaches, *"as a man thinketh in his heart, so he is"* (Proverbs 23:7 KJV). I remember whining to my husband that I was not happy. He said, "Jean, if you would learn to make yourself happy, I think I could help make you happier." I remember thinking that was silly. I believed my "knight in shining armor" was all I needed to be happy and content. Therefore it followed that if I was not happy, it was not my fault; it was my knight's fault. I have since learned that there is no human being on this earth who can fill all my needs. There are no "knights in shining armor." There are human beings who fall in love and share life, but each person is responsible for his or her own life. I am to live life for the Lord God and share my life with others. One past mistake I made was living life for my loved ones. Today I would give my life for my loved ones, but I do not live life for them.

There are people who have been victimized over and over. It seems natural for a time to focus on those who inflicted this pain. However, there comes a time when we must rid ourselves of this baggage. How? We tend to think, "That can't be done!" Yes it can, but first we have to do the *difficult*.

The *difficult* is bringing to mind all the pain I carry through life. Some of us think that our pain is worse than anyone else's. That is "victim" thinking. Some people have a victim living within them, who victimizes again every time hurtful memories surface.

Now I realize that people must take charge of their thinking and bring their pain into the open for the purpose of getting healthy. First, identify the hurt. I ask, "Did I deserve to be wounded by this person?" The answer is, "No, I did not." This person hurt me because of who he is, not because of who I am. Hurting people hurt people. This is truth, and another promise from God comes to pass, "*Then you will know the truth, and the truth will set you free*" (John 8:32 NIV). I am learning that if I walk in the truth, I will walk in wellness. I will not be afraid.

Chapter 6

VICTIMIZATION

To be victimized in any way has the potential to leave a person feeling "less than." For me, one of the most devastating effects of being victimized was taking on the shame of the abuser by thinking I had somehow caused the abuse. This feeling left me with the attitude of a victim. When someone hurt me, it seemed acceptable. In my recovery I learned about boundaries and that I had the right to protect myself. When I had a mind-set of "less than," I did not realize the reality of the abuse. I was blessed to come in contact with people who were willing to help me, even though at the time I did not know that I needed help. Some of my issues were low self-esteem and thinking my feelings were not as important as others. My opinions and my needs lost value; I was not a good friend to myself. I constantly felt responsible for others and their feelings, always waiting for something to go wrong. With no personal relationship with the Lord Jesus Christ, and only "religion," I did not have God at the center of my life. I lived for my husband and my children, not for God. I was a sad, lonely person. Now I can cling to the affirmation that I am not a victim, I am a victor.

Like many other people, I often carried shame that did not belong to me; it belonged to the people who acted shamelessly. There will always be times when people hurt me, and there will be times when I hurt myself and others. But I realized that I had to stop the blaming. Only then could I mature and become honest in my thinking.

Is there a way of escape? The *difficult* is taking ownership of the pain. One may think something is not fair, and it probably is not. However, once a person has the pain, he or she owns it and cannot give it back. The only road I have found to health is to look at what the hurts have cost. Did the pain cost security, innocence, trust, self-esteem, relationships, hope, or dreams? Wounding results in many losses. A time comes when it is necessary to grieve the loss, prepare to let go, and begin the process of forgiving the one who did the wounding. For me, it was necessary to let go of the hurt before I was ready to deal with forgiveness.

Some may think forgiving is about forgetting. However, I found it impossible to forget some of the wounds from my childhood as well as some in my adult life. When I asked God to help me to forgive, He showed me what forgiving was about. God's command to forgive was for my well being, not for the other person who hurt me. That person would have to go to God for his or her own forgiveness. God showed me that by not forgiving, I kept myself in bondage. My mistaken belief was that if I forgave, I was somehow letting the other person off the hook. The Lord God showed me that the other person was never on any hook—I was on a hook and needed to be set free. That awareness could only come from the Most High God. I was a walking corpse, dead with resentment, who did not want to see the truth. That awareness made it easier for me to want to forgive. I learned how to become willing to go to God for help. The only way I have ever been able to forgive was to ask the Lord to do the *impossible*—to give me a heart of forgiveness. I had to choose to be obedient to His will and remember that I too had been forgiven for my wounding of others.

One of the tools that helped me reach forgiveness was the Lord's Prayer. *He said to them, "When you pray, say: 'Father, hallowed be your name, your kingdom come'* (Luke 11:2 NIV).... *'Forgive us our sins as we forgive those who have sinned against us' "* (Luke 11: 4 NIV). By not having forgiveness in my heart, I was asking the Lord not to forgive me. That was an eye opener!

Without the Lord, I was never able to truly forgive. I used to say the words, "I have forgiven," but in my heart I had not. With the grace of God, today I do truly forgive. I have learned that I am forgiven and I can be a forgiver.

Chapter 7

DEALING WITH RESENTMENTS

I have heard it said, "Holding onto resentments is like drinking poison, hoping someone else will die." That is self-destructive. Holding onto resentment is about hurting myself over and over. Feeling victimized often gave me an excuse to not look at my own issues.

Another aspect I learned about resentment was that my resentments were focused on my anger because my life was not the way I thought it should be. However, I found that resentments are disappointments turned into anger. If one does not express disappointment in a healthy way, those feelings turn into oppressive resentments.

I felt resentment for almost everything that happened to me. However, I did not realize how much I was filled with my unresolved anger. Then I learned that anger is the precursor to resentment. Had I been able to deal with my anger in a healthy way—by recognizing it, expressing it, and letting it go—I would have been doing what the Scriptures command me to do. *"In your anger do not sin: Do not let the sun go down while you are still angry" (Ephesians 4:26 NIV).*

As a child I was taught not to be angry, but in this Scripture, the Lord God says, "Be angry if necessary but do not hold on to it, for that is sin." Clearly He said this because expressing anger is human and in one's best interest. Without honesty, anger becomes destructive, and then there is the sin.

No doubt I was not honest with my feelings. My destructive thinking was both suicidal and homicidal. With a grateful heart to God, I never acted on my thinking. My resentments were costing me peace of mind, self-esteem, loving feelings, love of myself, and gratitude for what I really did have. My resentment caused me physical pain. I began to identify my anger before the sun set, as directed by Scripture. As often as I can, I let go of my anger. When I have difficulty letting go, I pray, and then I set a goal to take care of my emotional health and express myself whenever necessary.

I have learned that a person can become aware of the anger but not "stew" in it. Instead, I can seek to deal with anger in an appropriate way. A healthy way for me to handle anger and resentment is to do one or more of the following:

- If there is another person involved, express myself honestly with love.
- Write down my feelings and allow myself to feel them. Then let go of them.
- Go to the Most High God Himself. Share with Him how I feel and ask Him to take these feelings from me.

At one point on the road to health, I realized that my anger had not served me well. My anger had allowed me to hold onto things that hurt me and caused me to become the victim. I learned to control my emotions by thinking through what I was angry about. For me letting go of resentment was the *difficult*—I was making a decision to become healthy. By holding onto angry feelings, I was using up the energy that I could have been using for my personal growth.

Anger was the only emotion I could feel. Yet I was unable to express it, so it stayed inside me. No wonder I was depressed! My sadness seemed legitimate to me. I could never see myself as healthy, whatever I thought that was. The more I tried, the harder it got. Then I became more willing to learn to let go. That was the *difficult* for me: once again I had to become willing. Once I became willing, God did the *impossible*.

Today I believe that I am free of resentments. I pray to get to the place where I can always be honest about my feelings and begin to heal from resentment. I know that I am blessed of God, and that I can walk in His truth.

Chapter 8

SHAME

Shame is sometimes confused with guilt, but they are not the same. Shame can be a valid feeling as the result of something we have done. Shame can be a consequence due to a behavior or choice.

However, sometimes the shame does not belong to us. This shame is put upon us when someone acts shamelessly towards us. For example, when a person is sexually abused, he or she is left feeling the shame of this act. Indeed, in reality the shame belongs to the abuser, never to the victim. Yet people abused as children carry that shame into adulthood. The shame affects their self-esteem and, in the long run, the quality of their lives. People who take on that shame inevitably feel "less than."

Shame is the mindset that there is something "wrong" with me. Therefore, people develop masks to hide the belief that somehow they are a mistake. Of course, no one is a mistake. Perhaps, some people are convinced that they are mistakes because someone told them that. But remember what God said about his people in Psalm 139: 13-18 (NIV).

> For you created my inmost being; you knit me together in my mother's womb. I praise you because I am fearfully and wonderfully made; your works are wonderful, I know that full well. My frame was not hidden from you when I was made in the secret place.

> When I was woven together in the depths of the earth, your eyes saw my unformed body. All the days ordained for me were written in your book before one of them came to be. How precious to me are your thoughts, O God! How vast is the sum of them! Were I to count them, they would outnumber the grains of sand. When I awake, I am still with you.

Many shame-based people become convinced that they can earn God's love by doing and being perfect. God's love is freely given, not earned. Jesus never shames us. He allows each person to feel his or her guilt and shame. The world shames us, but He gives His peace.

When anyone goes to the Lord for forgiveness for shame, he or she will be set free. However, no person can ask for forgiveness for someone else's shame. Sometimes people try to do this. Each of us needs to identify what shame issues belong to us.

No one deserves to be abused, not by another person or by himself or herself. No matter what someone has done in the past, no one has the right to abuse anyone else.

"Therefore, there is now no condemnation for those who are in Christ Jesus" (Romans 8:1 NIV). *"Therefore, if anyone is in Christ, he is a new creation…"* (2 Corinthians 5:17 NIV).

Chapter 9

SEEING MYSELF THROUGH THE EYES OF OTHERS

Many of us have a distorted self-image. We see ourselves through other people's eyes, such as a critical parent, a negative teacher, or someone with condescending messages. When people believe these messages, they define themselves as "less than." On the other hand, if people are given lots of flattery, false praise, and ego boosts, they may come to believe they are "more than." Both are false messages that can hinder people in finding the true authentic self—that person whom God made us to be. Real people accept themselves for who they are. They love themselves, love their neighbors, and see themselves though God's eyes.

I can see that God has a plan for us. He said, "'For I know the plans I have for you,' declares the LORD, 'plans to prosper you and not to harm you, plans to give you hope *and a future'"* (Jeremiah 29:11 NIV). When I am in the midst of calamity, I have assurance that calamity is not God's plan for me. When I apply self-honesty in my life, I must apply it to this issue as well. I start by learning to accept who I am, realizing that no one is "less" or "more." Each person is different but not "more" or "less" than another. Seeing this helps me to begin to love myself. I see myself as someone God knew before I was born. *"Before I formed you in the womb, I knew you"* (Jeremiah 1:5 NIV). I show love to myself by being kind to myself. How? I stop criticizing and labeling myself with descriptors such as "I'm no good," "I'm lazy," "I can't do anything right," or "I'm worthless." One of the ways I have learned to stop labeling myself is to refrain from comparing myself to others. People never win when they compare themselves to others; it is a distorted view.

God wants me to enjoy life with the special talents He gave me. As I realize the value of who I am, I start to appreciate and respect myself and others for who they really are. Respect and appreciation for others comes with honesty about myself and without idolatry.

Being honest is the *difficult.* The *impossible* is seeing how deceived I have been to the truth; only God Himself can show me my deception. I can ask Him to show me, and He will.

I can now love myself as God made me. I have the grace to see how valuable I am to the Most High God and how valuable I am to His plan, *"Fear of man will prove to be a snare, but whoever trusts in the LORD is kept safe"* (Proverbs 29:25 NIV). When I am strong in the Lord, I can walk in the favor of God.

Chapter 10

LOVING MYSELF

"Love your neighbor as yourself."

—Romans 13:9 NIV

When I did not love myself, I did not love my neighbor. Now that I have learned to love myself, I love my neighbor.

My early life taught me contempt for myself. Not knowing this, I could not see that my thinking was unhealthy and assumed that I thought the same way as everyone else. When I started on the road to recovery, I became aware of self-love. Previously, I had believed that love of self was wrong. When I was young I was told not to look at myself in the mirror for more than a minute. Confident people were described as, "He loves himself so much, if he was chocolate he would eat himself." The message was always clear: do not love yourself. But God said, *"Love your neighbor as yourself"* (Matthew 19:19 and 22:39 NIV). I thought I loved my neighbor. But I discovered that I did not love me, so how could I love my neighbor? God Himself showed me that I am lovable because I am His. I started to appreciate and value my positive qualities. I asked God to help me with the parts of me that needed to be addressed and changed in me. I could almost hear Him say, "I have been waiting for you, my child."

I thought that I loved the way I was supposed to love—conditionally. Conditional love looks like this: *"If you do what I tell you to do, I will love you; if you will be who I want you to be, then I will love you; if you live by my rules, then I will love you. Remember: I know best."*

This love is twisted thinking and needed to be addressed if I was to become healthy. I had to unlearn what I believed. God showed me how to stop highlighting the broken parts of me. Sometimes He used the Word and sometimes He used other people. I stopped focusing on self-pity, inconsistency in my thinking, my need for approval, and my selfishness in not allowing other people to really know me.

On this journey, I eventually desired to be healthy. That proved to be the *difficult* for me because it took self-discipline for me to get there. To get well, I had let go of other people's issues. God sent the Holy Sprit to help me with this exactly when I needed it. I found He is always there. He taught me a helpful strategy: I take a deep breath and become aware that He is right here with me.

What did I need to do to allow myself to rest in Him? The visual in my head is a picture of Jesus walking with me on a grassy knoll. I put my hand in His. We walk and talk. What heavenly rest I find there.

The *impossible* for me was to be honest in everything. I had never been totally honest with myself. God did that part. He showed me how to be honest, and I finally listened. I learned that healthy people know how to ask for what they need. Now I am thankful for my life. I love me. I like me.

Respecting myself was a requirement to get on the road to health. How did I accomplish this? First, I realized that each person is worthy of respect. Some people are never taught how to respect themselves. Respect is *to be regarded with honor and esteem, a willingness to show consideration and appreciation.* I had to ask myself in all honesty, when was the last time I did that for me?

I believe we have to teach people how to treat us. In the past I gave others the message that it is all right for them not to respect me. I did not say it, but I acted as though it was acceptable. I never learned to protect my well-being or stand up for myself if I was mistreated. I did not even realize that I was not taking care of me. I was unaware that healthy people took care of themselves emotionally as well as physically. Therefore, I settled for unacceptable behavior and disrespect from others.

Today I believe that there are many ways for me to show respect to myself. I do this by being consistent, honest, courteous, kind, and through a host of other qualities that I value in myself. All of God's creation deserves respect, and I am a part of His creation—so is everyone else.

I have a God-given right to protect and take care of myself. When I taught others to treat me in a disrespectful way, I was being dishonest with my feelings. When I allowed myself to be used, I became a human doormat, someone who allows others to mistreat them without protest. That was where dishonesty with my feelings would show. To be willfully mistreated and not protest is foolish. This behavior can be a direct result of a low self-esteem. Now I know that no one is "more" or "less" than anyone else. No one has the right to mistreat anyone else and no one deserves to be abused. I now ask God to send His Holy Spirit to help me to take care of me. It is so much easier to take a stand for myself when I have already asked God to give me the strength I need. *"If you are wise, your wisdom will reward you; if you are a mocker, you alone will suffer"* (Proverbs 9:12 NIV).

I had to come to the place where I could see if I was allowing disrespect in my life. I had to become willing for the Lord to renew my mind. *"Do not conform any longer to the pattern of this world, but be transformed by the renewing of your mind"* (Romans 12:2 NIV). That was the *difficult*. I had to trust Him to do that. I had to believe that God is trustworthy, unlike many earthly fathers. In this world, some fathers show their children who God is by the way they live their lives and by the way they honor God. That is a wondrous sight to behold. Then there are fathers who do not know God themselves. Some fathers even abandon their children. A truth that is shared by people in recovery is that when a father is out of place, a mother gets displaced, children get misplaced, and God gets replaced.

So often in my work as a counselor I try to help others to remember that God is well able to restore us. The *difficult* is to become willing to allow God to do it. The *impossible* is restoration by the Most High God. There is a blessed assurance that He will do it: *"Ask and it will be given to you"* (Matthew 7:7 NIV).

Chapter 11

MY GOD/OUR GOD

"All things work to the good for those who love God and are called according to His purpose."

—Romans 8:28

One of the lessons I learned about God early in my recovery (from codependency) was so encouraging to me. I questioned why we were expected to praise God so much (you can see I did not know God yet). While listening to the 700 Club one night, someone asked Pat Robertson that very question. His answer spoke directly to my heart and told me who God was. Here is Pat's answer: "God inhabits the praises of His people, so when we praise Him, He is right there with us. The more we praise Him, the more we become like Him." How exciting! I then understood that everything God does for us, is for our good. Even the praise we give Him, He uses it to give us the blessing of His presence. That is when I started to learn about God's heart. So now I understand what it means to love and trust Him. I praise Him as much as I possibly can. *"Take delight in the Lord and He will give you the desires of your heart"* (Psalms 37:4).

Chapter 12

UNREALISTIC EXPECTATIONS

I had unrealistic expectations of other people. Wanting others to be what I desired them to be so that I could feel comfortable and expecting others to meet my every need was unrealistic. In fact, expecting the world to be all I want it to be is unrealistic. This attitude is self-centered. What would happen to that other person's reality if he or she had to live according to my plan?

Some of my unrealistic expectations included expecting my husband to read my mind. I thought if he loved me, he would know what I wanted without my having to ask for it. Another was expecting him to agree with me and not to disagree about anything. Another was expecting him to always be in a happy mood; if he was not in a happy mood, I assumed it must be my fault.

Obviously I had unrealistic expectations for myself as well as for others.

I found that anger and/or disappointment resulted when my expectations of someone or something went unmet or fell short. This is where the *difficult* came in. I realized that I was responsible for my own feelings, behaviors, and happiness. I remember the first time I heard that I was responsible for my own feelings. I thought, "That's silly! How can I be responsible when he made me feel like this?" Then I discovered that I choose how I feel. I did not like this idea at first, but it eventually set me free from allowing other people to be in charge of my feelings, *"Then you will know the truth, and the truth will set you free"* (John 8:32 NIV).

God did a mighty work in me when He showed me my own issues. I began to see that I was my own worst enemy. When God revealed to me that I had unhealthy thinking patterns, I had to deal with myself first. Again I asked God to help me with this. He showed me how to have the courage to ask for what I needed.

I stopped expecting everyone to agree with me. Now I see that I feared conflict. Since I never disagreed with anyone, I did not want anyone disagreeing with me. I thought the person did not love me if he or she disagreed with me. I now know that disagreement is not about love but about expressing oneself. Proverbs 29:25 (NIV) comes to mind, *"Fear of man will prove to be a snare, but whoever trusts in the LORD is kept safe."*

One of the most difficult things for me to do was to come to terms with accepting the way others are. However, I learned that a key to emotional health is accepting reality. I do not have to like it or in any way agree with it, but I cannot deny what is reality.

Acceptance is most difficult when the reality is not pleasant. Accepting the things I cannot change is mandatory for my emotional wellness. If I cannot change something, why do I spend energy worrying about it? A better and healthier approach is to learn to pray about it.

When I am struggling to deal with a difficult issue in my life, I try to identify the concern. If I am having a hard time identifying, if it is my issue, I have learned a strategy that helps. I write down my issue. Then I ask, does it belong to me? Is it about me or am I worrying about someone else's issue?

When I identify who owns the issue, I have a choice. If it is my issue, only I can deal with it and can decide what to do about it. I can try to change it on my own. If that does not work, I can turn it over to the Lord God to change it for me. This is a great faith builder.

If the issue belongs to someone else, and his or her sin or behavior is bothering me, nothing I can do will change it. However, I can learn from this opportunity by praying about it. I can turn my concern over to God for resolution and let go of it. I have found that an unproductive strategy is to keep doing the same thing over and over, expecting different results. If nothing changes, nothing changes. Something I have learned along the way is that I just cannot do some things; if they are going to be done, only the Most High God can do them.

Another benefit of letting go and accepting reality is the freedom that I find in learning to learn to live abundantly: *"I have come that you may have life, and have it to the full"* (John 10:10 NIV).

I have learned to pray, "Father, I am struggling with an unidentified issue and am having difficulty letting go of another person's issue, I pray that You by Your Holy Spirit will minister to my need and the needs of others. I thank You, Lord, for your faithfulness and for letting me know that I can come to You."

Something I have come to understand is the truth of the Scripture, *"I tell you the truth, whatever you bind on earth will be bound in heaven, and whatever you loose on earth will be loosed in heaven"* (Matthew 18:18 NIV). I have seen the results in my own life when I have been able to "loose" something or someone I had "bound" up by trying to control the situation myself. Healthy results occurred after a short wait. *God grant me the serenity to accept the things I cannot change.* If it is not my issue, then I must let it go. If I want to be emotionally and spiritually healthy, I must accept the reality that this issue is not mine.

I have long thought that when things were unbearable, my concerns belonged to someone else. I did not have the grace to deal with them. Maybe this was because they were not mine to deal with anyway.

The following verse speaks of idolatry. The apostle Paul tells us not to love or venerate anything more than God. If I look at my behavior honestly, sometimes I do just that. I make someone or something the center of my life; God has clearly told me that He is to be the center of my life. When I accept the reality of another person's issue and allow the other person to own his or her behaviors, I feel free. Then even more confirmation occurs that the Scriptures are absolutely true. Many times the above Scripture confused me because there were times when my life was unbearable. I always felt guilty that I could not see how this Scripture applied. Now it is clear! I did not have the correct information about emotional health. I was taking responsibility for another's sin. It does not make sense to repeat this action when I find the truth. I stand in absolute awe of the truth the Lord God has taught me. Now I can help other people without being in charge of them.

Chapter 13

JUDGMENT

"Do not judge or you too will be judged."
—Matthew 7:1 NIV

Through the years, I learned that when I judged the defects in others, I began to see them in myself as well. There are two parts to judgment. First, there is the sin of judging, for indeed who am I to presume to be in the position to judge anyone? I own that sin if I find myself in a judgment mode. Second, there is the damage I can do to others by judging them. When people receive the judgments of other people as truth, emotional wounds can result. Who is capable of judging another human being? (I am referring to the person, not the behaviors.)

The Scriptures tell us we will know them by their fruits, *"By their fruit you will recognize them. Do people pick grapes from thornbushes, or figs from thistles?"* (Matthew 7:16 NIV). So we are free to identify the fruits of the behaviors but not judge the person. When I find myself judging others, I quickly repent lest the judgment should come back on me. Jesus said,

> *"How can you say to your brother, 'Brother, let me take the speck out of your eye,' when you yourself fail to see the plank in your own eye? You hypocrite, first take the plank out of your eye, and then you will see clearly to remove the speck from your brother's eye."*
>
> —Luke 6:42 NIV

Judgment is a thief that steals my freedom to love. How can I have a loving relationship with another if I am busy judging? To judge, I would have to be "more than." I would have to believe that I know the answer to everything and assume wisdom to judge another. In the realm of Christianity, I have been commanded not to judge others. However, I can have the gift of discernment. But I am to use this gift to make healthy decisions for myself. This would be a godly thing for the head of a household to use to protect his or her family. The *difficult* would be disciplining ourselves not to judge. The *impossible* would be turning the judgment into love for others. That is what the Most High God can do for us.

Chapter 14

STEALING BLESSINGS

Scripture says, *"You shall not steal"* (Exodus 20:15 NIV). When I say, "I don't steal," I might think I am being truthful, but I may not be honest. Quite often I steal other people's blessing.

For example, when a child has homework to do, perhaps he has not completed it and time is passing. Does the adult do it for him by giving the answers? The parent has not blessed the child but stolen his blessing of failing. Yes, that's right—their blessing of failing. Failing can be a blessing. Sometimes people need to fail so that they can learn to take life seriously. There are also times when I steal the blessing of accomplishment. When I do something for others that they can do for themselves, I keep them from experiencing the blessing of being able to do it by themselves.

Some adults are spiritual babies who never learned to turn to God for help. They just turned to mom, dad, spouse, or whoever enabled them. I have to check my motives for why I provide help. Is it to please God or is it to make my life more comfortable?

In this context, enabling is not of God. Unlike "helping" another, enabling is taking another's responsibility so I, the enabler, will be more pleasing. Enablers kill the people they love—not physically, but definitely spiritually and emotionally. They can even steal the potential from loved ones by continually doing for them what they need to be doing for themselves. Most of the time the enabled demands and expects to be enabled. This is one of the ropes of bondage that the enabler must examine. Enabling is very costly to the one doing the enabling, stealing both identity and freedom.

When I see myself in this scenario and believe I have been stealing other's blessings by calling it love, I have to go to the Lord God with my concern. Love is a good thing, but enabling is not. People who genuinely help others, do it in obedience and because they have a heart of mercy given by God. They rarely have another agenda.

I am not saying I should not be helpful. Indeed, I am called to be helpful. But I must be careful not to damage others or steal their blessings with my attempts to help. If someone is in genuine need, as a Christian I must minister to the needy. What I must avoid is doing for others what they can do for themselves, hoping to receive love just because I did it.

Being honest with myself, and even challenging some of my own thinking, is the *difficult*. I can learn not to believe what I have previously believed. Having the strength to say "no" if I want to and not feel guilty is the *impossible*. The Lord God helps me with that. He teaches me to do the right thing for the right reason.

Chapter 15

How to Be Real

What are some of the masks people use to hide who they are or because they do not know who they are? Some common masks include false confidence, sweetness, niceness, kindness, and superiority, to name a few. I did not realize how much I used masks until I became real. How did I become real? To be real I had to be honest with myself and with others. To be real I had to accept myself and accept others for who they are.

If people do not learn for themselves how to overcome, how can they survive? If we do not learn the need for guidance from the Holy One, who made us, how are we going to survive? How can we live life to the fullest by being what God intended us to be?

I have learned that we are human beings not human doings. This means being the best I can be, not doing the best I can do. How I perform differs from day to day. Some days I perform well, but other days I do not. However, I can still be the best I can be. I cannot depend on my performance to define who I am. For example, what would happen if I found myself paralyzed and could no longer function the way I do now? Would I be worthless? The truth is no, I would still be me, a person of value. If it turns out I can no longer do what I used to do, that is all it means—I cannot do what I used to do. I am still who I am. Some of God's best warriors have had crippling things happen to them. When I think of them, I think of great prayer warriors who are so real.

The *difficult* is becoming willing to be real, to stop being a performer, and allow the Lord God to do the *impossible*—make me a new me. Who did God make me to be? Whoever I am, I do not need masks to hide myself. I do not need to be afraid people will find out who I am. I will be the authentic me and be all that I can be. I will be free.

I believe we all need to have a safe person in our lives with whom we can talk. Then we can learn to be a safe person for others. A safe person listens to my concerns or confessions without judging or attempting to fix me, yet still loves me. A safe person puts my secrets into her heart, and the only one she talks to about my secret is the Most High God. A safe person knows how to be a prayer warrior on my behalf. Having a safe person to talk to is a blessing. Being a safe person is another blessing. There are many blessings when I walk in faith with the Lord Jesus Christ. I know that I am a child of the King.

Having an attitude of gratitude is like taking spiritual vitamins every day. I am grateful for who I am and for all that I have been given. Even the painful issues in my life can be blessings and make me stronger. As I look around and see the world I live in, I say, "Thank you, Father, for what You have given me." I have a healthy respect for who the Lord God is and realize how my life could be so much more painful. I thank Him that He has given me a way of escape from the past.

My dad, who had only one leg, taught me to have an attitude of gratitude. At age seven, he lost one of his legs. He told his children not to be sorry he only had one leg but to be grateful that he did have one leg. My dad had an attitude of gratitude. I say I know God, yet I complain and murmur about what I do not have and think I should have. How can I know God and still complain and murmur?

When I enjoy what I have been given and do not groan about what I have not been given, I have everything I need to be the real me—all given by God. If people really take an honest look at some of the shows on television and stories in the newspapers, how can they not be grateful for their own lives? I am so grateful for my life. When I apply some of the truths I've discussed here, I feel grateful for who I am. I pray that everyone will find a more thankful heart and a more joyful life in Him.

Chapter 16

GRACE FOR TODAY

What does "grace for today" mean? I have been promised enough grace for today, a supply that I am supposed to live within. God said, *"My grace is sufficient for you"* (2 Corinthians 12:9 NIV). I know His grace is sufficient; I experience it every day.

Grace is power that strengthens life. The Scriptures say, *"You who are trying to be justified by law have been alienated from Christ; you have fallen away from grace"* (Galatians 5:4 NIV). We are responsible to stand fast and not fall from grace. As human beings, we need all of God's grace.

God has told me that He is by my side. If God is for me, who can be against me? In our vernacular, "Who cares?" Who is against me does not matter because God is for me. As a believer in Christ, I have everything that

I need to live life and live it to the fullest. Jesus said, *"...I have come that you might have life and have it to the full"* (John 10:10 NIV). Blessed with abundant life, I feel more deeply, am more aware of God, am more aware of blessings, and seem to have more of everything—more joy, more laugher, and more awareness. His abundance never ends.

John 10:10 (NIV), says *"The thief comes only to steal and kill and destroy..."* What better deception could the enemy use than addiction? This Scripture continues, *"I have come that they might have life and have it to the full."* His Grace is apparent once again. I have a Tower to run to. My God is my Tower.

The Bible assures me that, *"And we know that in all things God works for the good of those who love him, who have been called according to his purpose"* (Romans 8:28 NIV).

One of the many lessons I learned about God early in my recovery so encouraged me. I used to question why I was expected to praise God so much. While listening to *The 700 Club* one night, I heard someone ask Pat Robertson that question. His answer spoke to my heart and told me who God was.

He said, as I recall it, "The Scriptures say God inhabits the praises of His people, so when we praise Him, He is right there with us. The more we praise Him, the more we become like Him." How exciting! I then understood that everything God does is for our good. Even through the praise we give Him, He uses it to give us the blessing of His presence. That is when I started to learn about God's heart. So now I understand what it means to love and trust Him. I praise Him all the time. *"Delight yourself in the Lord and He will give you the desires of your heart"* (Psalms 37:4 NIV). I know that God loves me. He is so good to me.

I did not fully understand what the Scripture, *"And I will restore to you the years that the locust hath eaten,"* meant until someone set fire to our house and we lost most of our belongings. Our choices were to rebuild the house and sell it or rebuild and keep it. I heard the Lord say, "And *I will restore to you the years that the locusts hath eaten*" (Joel 2:25 KJV). We opted to keep our house. Within a year the house was better than it had previously been and built better than its original state. I received gifts from friends to replace items I lost in the fire. Some friends even gave us items they did not know were lost in the fire. I knew God was with us.

I have experienced additional touches from the Lord. He restored many areas of my life, including my self-esteem, my emotional health, my spiritual well-being, many physical conditions, and my relationships. One particular restored relationship was with my mum. We had an unspoken tension between us for forty years. Then, a few years ago, I went home to Scotland for a visit. The Lord did a mighty work. My mum and I connected, and I fell in love with my mum. We shared a spiritual connection. She told me I was a lovely woman and she liked me, words I had longed to hear. I felt as if a missing piece of my life was finally in place. God had restored a relationship once again.

Two years later, my mum went home to be with the Lord. I was asked to speak at her funeral and gave testimony that she had taught me about Jesus when I was a child. Because she did, I was able to recognize Him when I met Him.

I still feel sad for all the years the locust had eaten, taking away from my relationship with my mum. I regret not being connected all those years. However, I own that and am most grateful for the wonderful times I spent with her. God magnified the time we did have.

"I will restore to you the years the locusts have eaten..." (Joel 2:25 KJV). He spoke the truth: "I will restore all that the locusts have stolen from you," and God did. My prayer for others is to see Him restore ALL that the locusts have stolen from them. Today I can say, I am happy. I am well. I love life.

Chapter 17

PARENTING

"Blessed is the man who has a quiver full of children."
—Psalm 127:5 NIV

Jesus said, *"Let the little children come to me"* (Matthew 19:14 NIV). In this Scripture, I believe He is saying, "...do not do anything that will harm these babies in any way or stop these children from coming to Jesus." I believe He expects us to parent the way He does.

I have been given everything I need to do that. When I received spiritual and emotional health, I became a better parent. God opened my heart and my eyes so I could experience the joy of parenting in the Lord.

Many words are written on the subject of parenting, with varying opinions offered. But what does God say about parenting? After all, His instruction and opinion is the only one that counts. God said children are a gift to us from Him. He tells us He requires us to teach our children about Him, their Creator:

> *"These commandments that I give you today are to be upon your hearts. Impress them on your children. Talk about them when you sit at home and when you walk along the road, when you lie down and when you get up."*
>
> —Deuteronomy 6:6-7 NIV

He also said parents should nurture their children:

> *"Fathers, do not exasperate your children; instead, bring them up in the training and instruction of the Lord."*
>
> —Ephesians 6:4 NIV

Children must obey their parents:
> *"Children, obey your parents in everything, for this pleases the Lord."*
>
> —Colossians 3:20 NIV

There are many blessings for parents when both children and parents learn to obey God's Word. God said:

> *"Honor your father and your mother, so that you may live long in the land the LORD your God is giving you."*
>
> —Exodus 20:12 NIV

What a wonderful promise!

How can parents be obedient to the Father in parenting their children? Some of what I learned about parenting came by following God's example—watching how God parents me. We are children of God, and children of God should imitate God:

> *"Be imitators of God, therefore, as dearly loved children."*
>
> —Ephesians: 5:1 NIV

God has shown me that He is on my side and will always be there for me. He has clearly taught me that He will always let me suffer the consequences of my choices. He has taught me to come under His authority. He has no desire to control me but does desire for His people to come under His authority. I have found that is where I am blessed and safe. He wants His people to be what He created them to be. That is where I found wholeness.

Look at some ways we humans try to parent. Some of us have tried yelling, punishing, shaming, controlling, ultimatums, and enabling. Some of us have tried being friends with our children. We can be friends to our children, but not exclusively. First we are the parent, in the position of willingly taking authority over our children.

Although control may mimic authority, it is ineffective. Control is motivated by wanting things done our way. On the other hand, authority is motivated by what is best for the whole family. When parents are dealing with their children, their authority is God-given. Like the Lord God, we are willing to do what is best for our children. Here are some behaviors I have witnessed. Mothers and fathers who have unresolved problems with each other can be guilty of not standing as one unit when it comes to the parenting of the children. When that happens, the children learn to manipulate the parents. They play their parents against each other. If the authority in a family is not consistent, the child is the one who suffers the most. Mom and Dad must be in agreement regarding their value system, including parental discipline.

To be healthy, discipline should not be a *reaction* to an unacceptable behavior but a *response* to an unacceptable behavior. Never shame a child. I have seen parents in public places such as supermarkets shame their children for an innocent accident. Instead, that would be the perfect time to nurture a child and assure him that accidents happen to everyone. This is a perfect time to show a child that we are on his or her side. I see my daughters act this way consistently with their children, and I am delighted.

A healthy strategy is to have rules and values in a family and to establish consequences for the rules and values that are disregarded by the child. However, it is important to make sure the consequences fit the act. This is a way we can imitate God.

> *"Be imitators of God, therefore, as dearly loved children."*
>
> —Ephesians 5:1 NIV

At all costs I must be consistent so I can establish stability.

Parenthood is definitely a most important ministry given to us from God. He will provide what we need as parents if we seek Him. *"Ask and it shall be given you. Seek and you will find; knock and the door will be opened to you"* (Matthew 7:7 NIV).

Parenting suggestions that I have learned:

1. Teach children about God by letting them know they are a gift to you from God.

    > *"These commandments that I give you today are to be upon your hearts. Impress them on your children. Talk about them when you sit at home and when you walk along the road, when you lie down and when you get up."*
    >
    > —Deuteronomy 6:6-7 NIV

2. Nurture children by teaching them they are valuable and lovable.

3. Learn how God loves and treats you. You will then be able to love and treat your children in a healthy way. Christians imitate God. Do it His way.

4. Give up the desire to control your children, trying to make them do what you want them to do. Is it the right and healthy thing to do, or is it because it would make your life easier? This is a behavior to be examined.

5. Love your spouse. Respect each other. Be a healthy and godly role model for your children.

6. Do not provoke your children. *"Fathers, do not embitter your children, or they will become discouraged"* (Colossians 3:21 NIV).

7. Show your children who God is by imitating God.

I have also learned the difference between healthy and unhealthy behavior.

Unhealthy	Healthy
1. Inconsistent messages	Consistent in their beliefs
2. Keeping secrets	Open—Honest
3. Miscommunication	Communicates clearly
4. No boundaries	Healthy boundaries

5. No confrontation	Confrontation in love
6. Need others to validate them	Know their own value
7. Does not express feelings, (i.e. anger goes unexpressed or "stuffed")	Encouraged to express feelings
8. Fight as if there is something threatening their lives	Feels safe enough to disagree
9. Blaming	Take responsibility for their own actions
10. Feel they should have their needs met without stating needs	Able to ask for what they need
11. Different rules for different family members	Same rules for the whole family.
12. Experience conditional love (i.e, "if you do this, I will love you.")	"I love you no matter what."

The apostle Paul wrote, *"Whatever you have learned or received or heard from me, or seen in me, put it into practice. And the God of peace will be with you"* (Philippians 4:9 NIV).

Chapter 18

TWELVE STEPS OF RECOVERY

1. We admitted we were powerless over alcohol, drugs, and many other destructive behaviors— that our lives had become unmanageable.

    "I know that nothing good lives in me, that is, in my sinful nature. For I have the desire to do what is good, but I cannot carry it out."
    —Romans 7:18 NIV

Admitting that our lives have become unmanageable is the first healthy piece of awareness we probably have had in some time. Admitting we are powerless is not an easy process. We must recognize that alcohol, drugs, and/or any other things we may be abusing are bigger than we are. We only have to be honest about how many times we promised ourselves to stop the abuse but then found ourselves looking for a reason to return to our past abusive behaviors. When we can honestly see our lives have become unmanageable, we find that the trouble is in our lives: broken relationships, job losses, spiritual bankruptcy, and quite possibly physical or legal problems. That reflects this Scripture, "I know that nothing good lives in me, that is, in my sinful nature. For I have the desire to do what is good, but I cannot carry it out" (Romans 7:18 NIV). But there is a way of escape!

2. We came to believe Jesus Christ could restore us to sanity.

> *"Trust in the Lord with all your heart and lean not on your own understanding; in all your ways acknowledge Him, and He will make your paths straight."*
>
> —Proverbs 3:5-6 NIV

This step implies we have seen the insanity of our behavior. This is a good place for us to look at our behavior. Is it healthy? The truth is that Jesus Christ can restore us to sanity. He is the only one who is bigger than this disease. It takes the Most High God Himself to return us to sanity, to return us to a healthy lifestyle, and to truly know Him. Now we can have a lifestyle where we do not have to bully those we say we love. No more yelling at people, no more acting out, no more lying about where we have been or what we have been doing. With Jesus we can learn what is right and healthy—and do it.

3. We made a decision to turn our will and our lives over to the care of Jesus Christ.

> *"And without faith it is impossible to please God, because anyone who comes to Him, must believe that He exists and that He rewards those who earnestly seek Him."*
>
> —Hebrews 11:6 NIV

How Scripture leads us to healthy thinking and godly living is so encouraging! Of course we have to be honest about our own defects and become willing to let God change us to what He originally intended us to be. This means simply believing He is God and learning to do what He asks us to do. Then we can have all the countless blessings He has for us.

4. We made a searching and fearless moral inventory of ourselves.

> *"Search me, O God, and know my heart, test me and know my anxious thoughts. See if there is any offensive way in me, and lead me in the way everlasting."*
>
> —Psalms 139:23-24 NIV

This step is the core of the recovery process. Without honesty, this process is not effective. "If you work the program, the program works." I know this to be true in my own experience. If we only put fifty percent effort in, we only get fifty percent return. Give all our effort to recovery and He will honor our effort by giving us the power and strength to stay healthy.

5. We admitted to our heavenly Father, to ourselves, and to another human being the exact nature of our wrongs.

> *"Therefore confess your sins to each other, and pray for each other so that you may be healed…"*
> —James 5:16 NIV

Finding a person we trust to share our past behaviors with is very important. It is painful to talk to someone about our past and be judged for it. We must find someone who understands that we are all sinners, saved by God's grace. We must then do as the Scripture says: confess to each other and pray for each other. There is great power in sincere prayer. Here is a truth: He gives grace to the humble. To be humble can be a difficult thing to do, but remember: If you do the difficult, God will do the impossible. In addition, to be humble is the healthy thing to do.

6. We were entirely ready to have God remove all of our defects of character.

"I acknowledged my sin to you and did not cover up my iniquity. I said, 'I will confess my transgressions to the Lord'—and you forgave the guilt of my sin."

—Psalm 32:5 NIV

By this step we will be open to confess to the Lord God Himself. We thought about how free we would feel. We were willing to tell Him of our own free will what He already knows. Our will is the only thing we have that is ours. We needed to be willing to go to Him of our own free will.

7. We humbly asked Him to remove our shortcomings.

"If we confess our sins, He is faithful and just and will forgive us our sins and purify us from all unrighteousness."

—1 John 1:9 NIV

When we asked the Lord God to forgive us and received His forgiveness, we then accepted the realization that the Most High God had forgiven us. When He forgives us, we are forgiven. We could accept His forgiveness and know that we were totally forgiven. No other forgiveness even comes close to that—not ours, not any other person's. The Lord God forgives us but He does not take away our consequences. My consequences have been faith builders. Dealing with consequences made me turn to Him for help. He showed me how to deal with what I owned—consequences!

When He sets us free we are free indeed. When we ask for forgiveness but continue to think we are not worthy of forgiveness, then what we are saying to the Lord Jesus is, "What You did for me was not enough." If I believe that what He did was not enough, then I do not know Him.

8. We made a list of all persons we had harmed, and became willing to make amends to them all.

> *"Let no debt remain outstanding except the continuing debt to love one another."*
> —Romans 13:8 NIV

This healing step takes honesty to admit to the wounding we had done to other people. When we became willing to make amends, we had to proceed with care and humility. We had to take into consideration how other people may feel. We knew we might find angry responses from others. We did not make amends to get pats on the back; we did it because the Scripture tells us to. We did it because it was necessary for our spiritual well-being (which is one of the reasons the Scripture tells us to). It was also a way to let others know that we were truly repentant for what we had done to them. Truly, this was a healing step for us, for others, and for our relationships.

9. We made direct amends to such people whenever possible, except when to do so would injure them or others.

> *"Do not repay evil for evil. Be careful to do what is right in the eyes of everyone. If it is possible as far as it depends on you, live at peace with everyone."*
> —Romans 12: 17-18 NIV

Direct amends were made to the person, face to face, if that was possible. Sometimes this needed to be done by telephone or in writing. The most important part was to be sincere. For example, in our addictive (sinful) behavior we were abusive either verbally or physically to our children; maybe we never went to any of their extra curricular events with them or to any of their activities.

Seeking to make amends looked like this: We took the time to express ourselves, as it was not effective to do it "on the run." We sat with our children and told them that we understood how much we had hurt them. We then let them know how sorry we were and made a commitment to not behave like that again. It has been said, "An amend is an apology with a promise not to do it again."

Another option is indirect amends. As the step states "except when to do so," we may find ourselves in a situation where it would be hurtful to another person if we made direct amends to someone else, and this other person was involved in some way. This would be a time when an indirect amend would be the direction to take. Some examples of indirect amends are giving to a charity on behalf of someone or doing a kindness for someone else. This is a good time for us to remember 1 John 1:9 (NIV), *"If we confess our sins, He is faithful and just and will forgive us our sins and purify us from all unrighteousness."*

10. We continued to take personal inventory and when we were wrong promptly admit it.

> *"Let us examine our ways and test them, and let us return to the Lord."*
> —Lamentations 3:40 NIV

As we practiced these steps, we found this was a personal process. This was about spiritual maintenance on ourselves, and the end of justification and rationalization. We no longer needed to depend on those strategies as we learned to be honest. We were becoming real and had nothing to justify or rationalize. When we found ourselves tempted to be dishonest, we called on the Lord to help us. We found that He is only a breath away.

11. We sought through prayer and meditation to improve our relationship with Jesus Christ, praying only for knowledge of His will for us and for the power to carry it out.

> *"Do not conform any longer to the pattern of this world, but be transformed by the renewing of your mind. Then you will be able to test and approve what God's will is—His good, pleasing and perfect will."*
>
> —Romans 12:2 NIV

One way I learned about God's will for me was to read the Scriptures to see what God said about His desire and what I needed to learn. I learned that my will and God's will differ sometimes. Only when my will aligned with God's will did I find peace. I had to learn about God and how His will for me was the best for me. He wanted me to have an abundant life. Sometimes my will was not always in my best interest. Sometimes my will was to settle for unacceptable events. This was not what the Lord God desired for me. He taught me to believe that I belonged to Him. He wanted abundance for me—abundance in grace, joy, peace, love, knowledge of Him, and abundance in all things good. I began to see how exciting it was when I walked with Him.

12. Having had a spiritual awakening as a result of these steps, we carried this message to others, and practiced these principles in all our affairs.

> *"You my brothers, were called to be free. But, do not use your freedom to indulge the sinful nature, rather serve one another in love."*
> —Galatians 5:13 NIV

Truly these twelve steps were drawn from the Scriptures. Clearly, the Lord God has given addicted people a way of escape and a way back to Him. I have heard it said that there are two categories of Christians: the Christian who is a Christian because he or she does not want to go to hell, and the Christian who has been to hell and does not want to go back there. I discovered that if we are honest and willing, the Lord God will honor us as we continue to seek Him and His wisdom.

Now that we were walking in health and with the Lord Jesus, it was time for us to pass it on. We saw that we could help others through this experience. We could lead them to the truth, the Lord Jesus. His way is the truth. Now that we have learned to practice all of these principles (honesty, kindness, personal responsibility, fairness, respect, consideration for others), we have much more sober thinking in everything we do.

Chapter 19

TAKING A PERSONAL
INVENTORY

Below is a list of faults that I believe we as human beings share. The Lord God will shine His light on the ones we own when we ask Him. After identifying our faults, we can ask the Lord God to remove them. A willing heart is necessary to take an effective personal inventory.

FAULTS/DEFECTS/CHARACTER FLAWS

Dishonesty
Bitterness
Anger
Controlling
Selfishness
Judgmental attitude

Self-centeredness
Self-pity
Here are some of the indicators:

DISHONESTY: Not being honest about what we are feeling or what we are thinking, even with ourselves. For good emotional health, we must learn to name honest thoughts and feelings. Remember the truth shall set us free! One of the ways we can identify if we are being dishonest is to check if our thinking and our feelings are the same. If we are saying one thing and feeling another, we are being dishonest. We need to be clear about what we are feeling and express it. This includes positive as well as negative emotions.

BITTERNESS: Holding on to negative memories. Bitterness is one of the most destructive emotions anyone can feel. It can affect our physical well-being as well as our emotional and most certainly our spiritual well-being. Sometimes we can see bitterness on a person's countenance. Bitterness causes harshness in our interaction with others. One of the ways to identify if we are bitter is to check our attitude when we think of the experience that caused us to feel the bitterness in the first place. If we are bitter about anything, we are being shortchanged of joy and serenity. We can give ourselves the gift of well-being; we are the only ones who can. When we do the difficult, God will do the impossible. When we become willing to let it go, He will remove it!

ANGER: Holding onto feelings of anger because we are either hurt or disappointed. Being angry can be valid, but holding on to it is not. Anger is sometimes the end result of not getting what we want. The Lord God said, *"Do not let the sun go down while you are still angry"* (Ephesians 4:26 NIV). I hear Him say acknowledge the anger and deal with it. Express it if needed, or talk to a safe person about how you feel, and you will find it easier to let go.

CONTROLLING: Trying to make people live the way we think they should. How does that look? It looks like this: always telling the people in our lives what or how to do things and calling it suggestions. Generally if we can get others to do it our way, it makes us more fulfilled. Actually if we will control our own issues such as temper, selfishness, and/or controlling, we will find fulfillment. Telling other people how to do things implies that controllers know what is best for everyone.

SELFISHNESS: Putting our own wants first (not our needs but our wants). This happens when we are not sharing with others or letting them know who we are. We do this by not sharing what we feel or what we value. In addition, we can be selfish with our material things, not sharing with others the blessings we have been given. Selfishness causes people to isolate themselves. Selfish people are themselves the main focus in their life.

JUDGMENTAL ATTITUDE: Judging other people. The Lord God was clear about this. He said,

"Judge not, lest you be judged" (Matthew 7:1 NIV). When we consider that we are not qualified to judge any other human being, it becomes clear what the Lord God is telling us. Unless we want to be judged by the same standards we use, we had better stop. A general rule of judgmental people is to build themselves up. If they are judging someone else it makes them feel superior, when of course we know no one is superior to another. That is why the Lord God is the only one to judge. He is the only one superior.

SELF-CENTEREDNESS: Having an attitude that everything is about them. An example is when a person has a dinner date with a friend. But when that friend has a serious accident, the person's response is "Does this mean we can't have dinner?" This person shows no concern for the friend but is irritated that her own plans cannot be fulfilled. Self-centered people lack empathy. As Christians, God is to be the center of our lives. If we are self-centered, that would make us the god of our lives. Self-centeredness does not allow for real love of others. Self-centeredness is all about me, me, me. Christians claim to be Christ-centered, yet some of them are self-centered. How can that be? One of the signs of self-centeredness is worrying how everything is going to affect us and our plans, or having concern only for our own well-being.

SELF- PITY: Feeling sorry for ourselves. I found the most effective way to deal with self -pity was to learn to have an attitude of gratitude. It is hard to feel sorry for myself if I am enjoying life, and it is easy to enjoy life if I am grateful. I started looking at my life and identifying what I am grateful for. Self-pity is thinking we have it worse than everyone else. With self-pity, we think that we have been more hurt or disappointed than anyone else. A good way to overcome this kind of thinking is to look around at other people and their situations and see that we are not so bad off. Taking responsibility for our own emotional state is also very helpful.

The Most High God will shine His light where we need it to shine, and bless us in our honest search.

Chapter 20

SOME OF OUR GOD-GIVEN GIFTS

Galatians 3:28	We are equal in His eyes.
Galatians 4:47	We will receive a spiritual inheritance.
Romans 13:12	We have armor to protect us in war (spiritual war).
Psalm 37:23-24	God always holds His children.
Jeremiah 32:40	God's promises last forever.
Mark 1:15	Belief in God affects the way we live.
Genesis 2:7	God is the life giver.
Leviticus 26:3-5	God blesses those who obey Him.
Psalm 24:3-6	We are blessed when we worship God.
Psalm 103:1	Christians bless God through praise.

Ephesians 1:3	Salvation is our greatest blessing.
Deuteronomy 7:9	God cares for His people.
Matthew 5:4	God promises to comfort those who mourn.
Romans 9:1	Jesus' forgiveness clears our conscience.
Proverbs 18:15	God's word helps us…
Psalm 34:18	God heals those with broken hearts.
Genesis 15:1	God will protect us.
1 John 4:18	Love drives fear away.
James 2:23	We can be friends with God.
Psalm 32:5	God forgives and removes guilt.

All of these gifts and lots more have been given to God's people. If a person is one of God's people, he has many gifts. If someone is not yet one of God's people, he should know that when he comes to faith in Christ, there are many gifts waiting for him to receive.

Chapter 21

UNDERSTANDING ALCOHOLISM

The consequences of alcoholism are many and grave. Alcoholism is acknowledged by the American Medical Association (AMA) as a disease, meeting the criteria of progressive, chronic, and life threatening. Indeed, alcoholism steals one's quality of life.

Some people take issue with that diagnosis. However, given the truth of the condition some may be open to accepting the diagnosis definition. I believe the initial use of the alcohol/drug to medicate oneself is the sin. People look to drugs, alcohol, or any number of addictive behaviors to do what they should ask God to do: to fill that person up with His Spirit and take away the emptiness. This is the beginning of healthy healing.

The disease of addiction is apparent when the person no longer has any control over the use of the alcohol/

drug. The addicted person has either surrendered into bondage or been captured into bondage. How one got addicted does not matter once the person is addicted. The addicted person has been deceived. The alcohol, or whatever addictive behavior is present, is not the cure-all it was thought to be. In reality, it steals the addict's quality of life (physically, emotionally, spiritually), thinking process, and future unless intervention occurs. During this time, enablers can learn to replace enabling behaviors with prayer for intervention.

To learn to love in a healthy way means allowing the people in one's life to pay the consequences of their own sin, decisions, actions, or lack of responsibility. To continue to enable these people is stealing their blessing.

Chapter 22

UNDERSTANDING
CODEPENDENCY

Codependency is a condition that stops growth. It can happen if you come from an Alcoholic family, or any unhealthy background. One of the things that happens is, learning to stuff feelings, not even recognizing what we feel, which leads us to denial. If a codependent is in a relationship with an addict, the condition worsens. Codependents learn to make people the center of their lives, instead of God, even when we think we are "good Christians." I personally lost my identity in the days when I was co-dependent. People pleasing, accepting unacceptable behavior from loved ones, low self-esteem, focusing on others' problems instead of our own, giving of ourselves for the wrong reasons, blaming self for others problems, (i.e. if I was a better spouse he/she wouldn't do this). This leads to taking responsibility for other peoples' problems; that is not true, how can you be responsible for someone else's sin. Can you go to Heaven/Hell for someone else? Doesn't make sense when you see it clearly.

Of course one of the biggest areas in this disease is denial. I personally learned that denial kept me from growing.

Here is a list of behaviors that is good for codependents to learn.

Focus on self and the changes you want to make.

Find validation in the Lord God not your spouse or your job.

Stop fighting as if it were life-threatening. (if this is one of your behaviors).

Stop obsessing over the things that happen to you.

Start challenging some of your beliefs. i.e. be sweet, be pleasing. Replace it with "be honest." You may find you will be sweet and pleasing for the right reasons, not because you're scared not to.

Start trusting yourself. You are a child of the King!

Learn to get your priorities in order.

These things are intended to help you to be kind to yourself, and to take proper care of yourself. Remember God said; *"Love your neighbor as yourself."* (Romans 13:9).

I heard God saying He expected me to love myself and love others, that was when I heard permission to love myself.

Hope this will help you get started on the road to recovery.

Chapter 23

SOBRIETY

There is more to sobriety than not using the drug or behavior that a person may be addicted to. There is healthy thinking, sane thinking. The Word of God is the most effective way to attain healthy thinking and behavior.

There is love of God, love of self and love of others. There is an awareness of God's sovereignty.

He made us; it follows He would be the one who could restore us from whatever bondage we have been in.

Sobriety includes making up for all the behaviors you have had that have wounded others.

Be honest with self and ask the Lord God to help you see what addiction has cost you and those who love you.

If you want a personal relationship with the Lord God, then make amends to Him for your behaviors.

Be willing to humble yourself and let the people you have hurt know how much you regret the pain you have caused.

Be willing to make amends to yourself, for the many ways you have hurt yourself. Do you know that making amends is apologizing with a promise not to do it again.

Sobriety also includes an extraordinary amount of gratitude to The Most High God for salvation.

Gratitude for your new way of thinking, for your new awareness of God and all the things He has shown you, like freedom to be real, to be honest, to be the best you.

The ability to let go of all the things you hold on to that may keep you in bondage of a sort. That would include, people, places and things. A willingness to be the best you can be. To be willing to acknowledge that addictive thinking is twisted. Twisted thinking is often motivated by egotism. I have heard it said around 12 step programs; "The definition of an egotist is; a self made man who worships his maker." Addictive thinking is the epitome of unhealthy thinking; it thinks it is always right; it is willing to go to any lengths to get what it wants. It follows, if you want to have healthy sobriety you must be willing to go to the same lengths to get healthy sobriety.

Sobriety is peaceful. Addiction has no peace.

Sobriety is being responsible. Addiction is irresponsible.

Sobriety can be filled with hope. Addiction is hopeless.

Sobriety helps you to be open to others. Addiction closes you down and helps you hide.

Sobriety is wellness. Addiction is sickness.

Sobriety has light. Addiction is dark.

I could go on and on there are many areas to cover. I encourage you to go on a search and find more positive aspects of your sobriety.

I pray your sobriety will bring you joy and peace which means a personal relationship with the Lord God.

Printed in the United States
64559LVS00001B/127